FRIENDS
OF ACPL

LET'S TALK ABOUT

FIGHTING

REVISED FOR EDUCATIONAL USE

By Joy Wilt Berry

Illustrated by John Costanza

CHILDRENS PRESS ™

CHICAGO

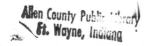

Let's talk about FIGHTING.

Fighting can be harmful.

When people fight:

They can hurt each other's bodies.

They can hurt each other's feelings.

They can break or ruin
each other's things.

When you are angry,
try not to hurt yourself or others.

Do not hit, kick, bite, scratch,
pinch, or pull anyone's hair.

When you are angry,
try not to break or ruin anything.

Try not to hit, kick, or throw things
that can be broken or ruined.

If you do not want to fight,
try to stay away from
anyone who makes you angry.

If you do not want to fight,
do not play too roughly.

Someone usually gets hurt
when people play roughly.

Often the person who has been hurt
gets angry and wants to fight.

If you do not want to fight,
do not spend too much time
with one person.

People who get tired of
being around each other
often fight.

15

If you do not want to fight,
ignore anyone who
calls you names or says mean things.

If someone wants to fight with you,
walk away.

If that person follows you,
ask an adult to help you.

You can solve the problems
you have with other people
without fighting.

If someone does something
that makes you angry,
do not do anything right away.

If you act too quickly,
you may get into a fight.

When you are angry,
slowly count to ten.
This will give you time
to calm down.

19

After you have calmed down,
talk with the person who has
made you angry.

Do not scream or call names.
Do not say bad things.

Talk about how you feel.

Explain why you are angry.

Tell the person
what you think should be done.

Give the other person
a chance to talk.

Listen carefully.

Show respect for
the other person's
thoughts and feelings.

Try to understand
the other side of the story.

THESE PENS ARE NOT ONLY YOURS. GRANDMA GAVE THEM TO BOTH OF US.

SHE'S RIGHT. GRANDMA DID GIVE THE PENS TO BOTH OF US. I FORGOT ABOUT THAT!

After the two of you
have said what needs to be said,
decide what to do.

There are many ways
to solve a problem:

You can do
what the other person
wants to do.

The other person
can do
what you want to do.

You both can give in a little
without giving in completely.
This is called *compromising.*

If the two of you
cannot decide what to do,
ask someone to help you.

Ask someone who is
old enough and wise enough
to be fair.

And then follow that person's advice.

Fighting can be harmful.

When people fight,
they can hurt each other
or break or ruin
each other's things.

It is best for everyone
when problems are solved
without fighting.

To be happy, treat others
the way you want to be treated.

Everyone is happier
when no one fights.

About the Author
Joy Berry is the author of more than 150 self-help books for children. She has advanced degrees and credentials in both education and human development and specializes in working with children from birth to twelve years of age. Joy is the founder of the Institute of Living Skills. She is the mother of a son, Christopher, and a daughter, Lisa.